Coming United States

Table of Contents

Getting Started 2

Deciding to Come 4

Making the Trip 8

Arriving at Ellis Island 12

Index 16

by Liz Ray

Getting Started

For many years, people have been coming to the United States from other places in the world. They leave the countries where they were born. They come here to live and work, and to make a new home. These people are called **immigrants**.

Millions of immigrants have come to the United States to start new lives. These people leave their homes, families, and friends behind. They try to rebuild their lives in a new country.

Ellis Island in 1920

Long ago, many immigrants arrived at **Ellis Island** in New York Harbor. The government used Ellis Island as a place for receiving immigrants. Let's find out more about Ellis Island and these immigrants.

Deciding to Come

The busiest years at Ellis Island were from 1892 to 1924. Many people came to the United States during those years. Why did they come? Where did they come from?

Immigrants came here for many reasons. Some people left their home countries because there was not enough food or land to support them. Others left because of wars or other problems.

Many immigrants came to the United States to find safety and freedom. We call these immigrants "refugees." They were afraid they would be mistreated, or harmed, if they stayed in their home countries.

Most people who arrived at Ellis Island came from **Europe**. They traveled across the Atlantic Ocean by ship. They came from many different countries such as Poland, Russia, and Italy.

Some of the immigrants who came here had special skills. For example, some were farmers, doctors, or shopkeepers. Some of the people had enough money to easily begin a new life. But many others came here with very little money and few personal things.

Making the Trip

If you were moving to a new country, what would you take with you? In the past, some immigrants had to leave many things behind. They might leave some family members, too. Often, there wasn't enough money for everyone to travel at the same time.

Sometimes husbands, fathers, or sons came to the United States first, by themselves. Then, when they had saved enough money, they would send for their families. Some families had to wait a long time to be together in the United States.

In the past, people came to the United States on **steamships**. Most of the immigrants had to stay on the lower decks. These decks were crowded and smelly. It was hard for people to stay clean and healthy.

Many immigrants brought food from home. They also ate potatoes, eggs, prunes, and other food served on the ship. They ate their meals on their small bunks or outside on the upper decks.

After about two weeks at sea, the ship would finally dock in New York Harbor. But the immigrants were not free to go anywhere. First, they had to ride on ferryboats to Ellis Island.

Arriving at Ellis Island

At Ellis Island, doctors checked the immigrants for diseases. If people were healthy, they could stay in the United States. People who were sick sometimes had to return to Europe. Most people were able to stay.

Government workers also asked the immigrants questions. The workers wanted to know where the immigrants came from and where they were going to live or work. Many immigrants spoke little or no English. They had a hard time answering the questions.

This is why the workers often made mistakes with the immigrants' names. Sometimes names were misspelled. Sometimes names were changed. Many immigrants were renamed at Ellis Island.

When the immigrants left Ellis Island, some of them stayed in New York City. Some went on to other cities. Often, they lived in crowded neighborhoods with other families from the same country.

Daily life was difficult for most of the people. They had to work hard. They had to learn the English language and new **customs**.

Take a look at the graph. It shows you where many immigrants came from before they arrived at Ellis Island.

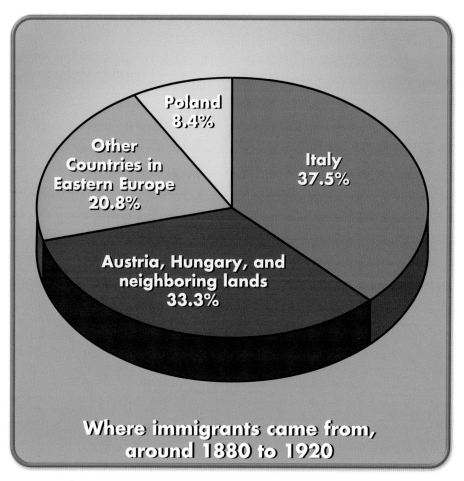

Poland
8.4%

Other
Countries in
Eastern Europe
20.8%

Italy
37.5%

Austria, Hungary, and
neighboring lands
33.3%

Where immigrants came from,
around 1880 to 1920

These new Americans are important to our **history**. All their hard work, hopes, dreams, and special customs helped to make the United States what it is today.

Index

country(ies), 2, 4–6, 8, 15

customs, 14, 15

Ellis Island, 3, 4, 6, 11–14

Europe, 6, 12, 15

family(ies), 2, 8, 14

ferryboats, 11

food, 4, 10

names, 13

New York City, 14

New York Harbor, 3, 11

steamships, 9

United States, 2, 4, 5, 8, 9, 12, 15